The Second E

CLUB RA

Myra & Bob Sawers
leaving the Chalamain Gap with the Larig Ghru in the background

Bob Sawers

British Library Cataloguing in Publication Data

Sawers Bob

The second book of Club Rambles Central and Southern Scotland.

1. Scotland - General

Acknowledgements

I should like to thank all the people who helped me with this book and supplied me with information. Special thanks to Myra for preparing the script, and to Charlie McCall and Jim Hannah for technical assistance, photographers Myra Sawers, Mike Callaghan, Billy Boyd, and Bill Goldie.

Once again Duncanrig Rambling Club rose to the challenge and completed all the walks in this book with great enthusiasm.

Front cover : The view from the disused Oban railway line looking towards

Glen Dochart (photograph by Mike Callaghan)

Printed by Bell and Bain Ltd., Glasgow

Contents

The Walks

Introduction

There has been in recent years an upsurge in the formation of walking clubs, all with their own concept of how a club should be run. There are multi-walk clubs and single walk clubs, the members should choose the type of walking pattern best suited to their club. Whichever type of walking pattern is used, all clubs have one thing in common - they are always on the lookout for routes.

I have assembled 25 walks covering central and southern Scotland, suitable for large walking groups of mixed ability. This is not a descriptive walking book, but is compiled to give basic information to allow a club route convener to prepare interesting and challenging walks.

The routes described make use of forestry paths, rights of way, landrover tracks and hill tracks. It should be remembered that many people rely on the land for a living, and damage to crops, livestock or property can affect their livelihood and can also lead to prosecution. Always keep the country code. Close all gates, do not foul water or trample crops, and respect game, wildlife and all growing things.

Ordnance survey maps should be used in conjunction with the information given in this book, and the ability to map read and use a compass is necessary. It is always best to research walks. The grading system used is an attempt to give an indication of the amount of effort required to complete a route. Please remember, however, that weather can greatly affect the difficulty of any route, also that each person's idea of degree of difficulty can be different. Therefore, the grades should be used only as a general guide.

Each group should have a leader and, where possible, a back-up leader, and also a designated back-marker, who should confer with the leader throughout the duration of the walk. Leaders should always make sure that members of his group are adequately equipped for the conditions on the day.

Preparation and research before the walk will ensure that the walk is enjoyable for everyone.

Take only memories, leave only footprints

SYMBOLS ON SKETCH MAPS

(S)	START OF WALK
(F)	FINISH OF WALK
→	ROUTE OF WALK
↟↟↟	UPHILL
▢	BUILDING
↟	PINE FOREST
ℜ	DECIDUOUS FOREST
〰	WATER
ʕ꞉ʒ	ROCKY FACE OF HILL
▲	SUMMIT
⅄	MAST
⚡	ELECTRICITY LINE
‡	RAILWAY
⊕	CHURCH
⋇	LIGHTHOUSE
⊓⊓	DAM
⊟	RAILWAY CUTTING

5

Location of Walks in Southern Scotland

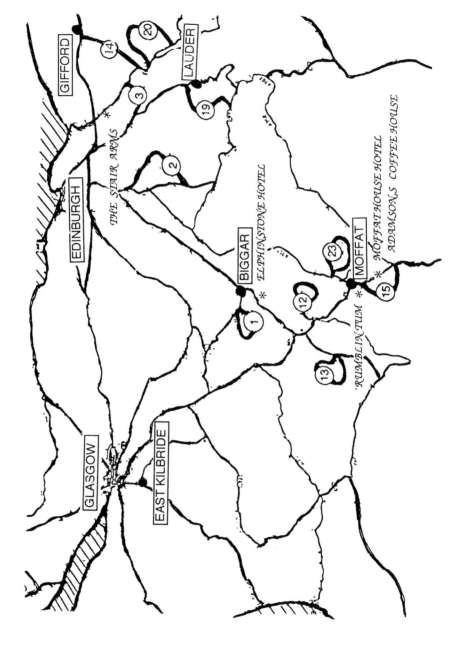

Location of Walks in Central Scotland

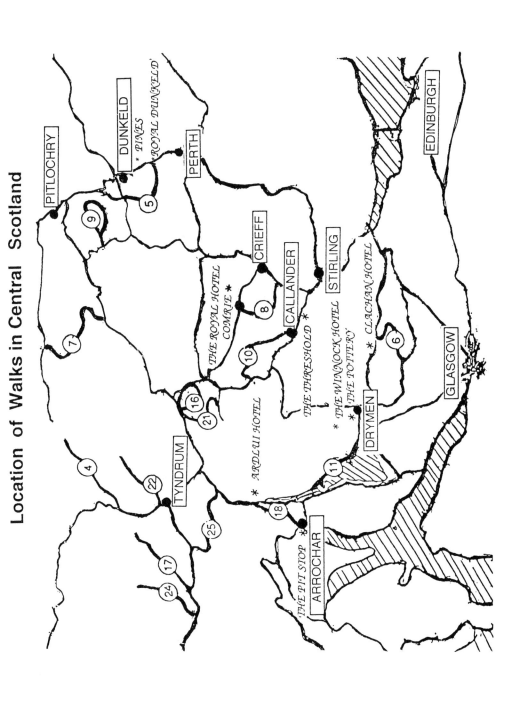

Notes

Route	Linear; start and finish identified.
Ordnance Survey	Relevant map number given.
Distance	In miles.
Comfort Stop	A location where public toilets are normally available.
Start Walk	Start identified by name and grid reference.
Finish Walk	Finish identified by name and grid reference.
Social Stop	A location where refreshments are normally available.
Description	Type of walk, e.g. forest, hill, river etc.
Walk Details	A short description of the route, highlighting particular points or directions.
Metalled Road	Distance walked on a made-up surface.
LRT	Distance walked on a landrover track or forestry road.
Trail	Distance walked on an area indicated by a single broken line on a map (the map may only indicate by a single broken line that it is possible to walk through that area - sometimes can be obscure).
No Trail	Distance walked over open, rough ground, normally by using a compass bearing.
Starting Height	Level in feet from the start of the walk.
Maximum Height	The highest point on the route.
Height Climbed	Not an accumulative figure, but the difference between the lowest and highest points on the route.
Bus Pick-Up Point	A location where it is possible for the bus to park.

Conditions in the countryside change; new forests are planted; fences are erected; new roads are laid, etc. So you may find variations from what is written in the text, but these should not prevent you from finding a way around them. While every endeavour has been made to be accurate in all details, should some errors have crept in I apologise in advance. No responsibility can be accepted for any loss etc. caused by inaccuracy, and the fact that a walk is described in this book does not guarantee that access will always be available.

Grading

The walks in this programme are graded as follows:

B+   **Moderate to Strenuous**. For the fit, usually over hilly and rough terrain. Height climbed 1,200 to 2,000 ft. Distance travelled 7 to 12 miles. Usually including several miles without trail.

B   **Moderate**. Average fitness required, usually over lower hills or undulating ground. Height climbed 600 to 1,200 ft. Distance travelled 7 to 11 miles. Usually including a short section without trail.

C+   **Easy to Moderate**. Requires average fitness, usually over undulating ground, and can include short uphill sections or rough ground. Height climbed 200 to 600 ft. Distance covered 7 to 10 miles.

C   **Easy**. Mainly level ground, usually on paths, tracks or minor roads. Height climbed not more than 200 ft. Distance travelled 7 to 12 miles.

It should be noted that the above gradings are intended as a rough guide. People have different ideas of degree of difficulty and the weather, ground conditions etc. on the day can have considerable effect on the walk. For further information contact the leader on any walk.

It should also be noted that a walk may be changed, due to perhaps adverse weather or ground conditions, or other good reason. Walkers must be properly equipped and competent for the grade of walk. Please note that walking boots are essential on 'B' walks and desirable on 'C' walks.

Duncanrig Rambling Club crossing the Chalamain Gap

Safety

The walks described in this book are not dangerous. There are no rock climbs, or raging torrents to cross. Nevertheless, mishaps do occur on the hills. Therefore it is advisable to take precautions.

* Don't go walking when unwell
* Always have proper clothing and kit
* Carry a first aid kit, whistle and torch
* Always carry food and drink
* Don't attempt to quicken natural pace in order to keep up with others
* Keep in touch with your companions at all times

All large parties should respond to a code of safety whistles:

One whistle blast	Stop
Two whistle blasts	Start
Repeated whistle blasts	Emergency

Preparations for Rambling

It is sometimes difficult to decide on what equipment to purchase. This section has been prepared to try to ease the problem. It is unwise to spend a lot of money on expensive equipment until you are sure good use will be made of the equipment.

Essential Items (Clothing)

* A sturdy pair of boots is advisable for all the walks as the terrain can get muddy or rough. All boots require protection such as waxing (see manufacturers' instructions).

* Wear two pairs of socks, one thin pair and one pair of rambling socks or stockings. Wear these when trying on boots for size.

* An old pair of trousers is quite suitable, provided they are strong and windproof. They should not be tight fitting. Jeans are not suitable as they do not dry out quickly.

* For very wet conditions, cheap overtrousers will break the worst of the weather, but condensation can be a problem. The more expensive type generally work better.

* A lightweight shirt or blouse

* A pullover or jumper should be taken or worn. Two thin layers are preferable to one heavy layer.

* The purpose of the top garment is to retain body heat. It should be closed by means of a zip, should have good pockets and a hood.

* A small woollen hat is fine for general wear and in winter a balaclava covering ears and chin. (In the summer a sun hat can be useful).

* Woollen gloves or waterproof mitts provide warmth.

Kit

Travel light if you can, but some kit is essential.

Rucksack   A small day pack with two side pockets is advisable. Most packs are not waterproof, therefore a good idea is to use a plastic bag to hold contents.

Map   Always take a suitable map of the area. An Ordnance Survey 1:50,000 Landranger Series is recommended. A transparent map case will protect it from the elements.

Compass   Essential, and know how to use it.

Route Card   Your intended route should be thoroughly researched and recorded on a route card.

Whistle   In an emergency it could save your life by indicating your position.

Torch   Especially in winter, a torch can be invaluable as darkness comes down so early and delays can occur.

Walking Stick   Can be useful in ascent and descent.

Ground Seat   Small padded or insulated square protects you from the cold when sitting.

First Aid   A small personal first aid kit should be carried.

Food and Drink   Some walkers like a good packed lunch, others eat little. However, it is advisable to have some sustenance. Carry it in a plastic box. Liquid could be tea, coffee or fruit juice. Hot water can be carried in a vacuum flask.

Dry Bag   A change of clothes can be left on the bus.

Tinto   (Walk 1)   *Photograph by Bob Sawers*

Summit of Tinto (Walk 1)   *Photograph by Bob Sawers*

Achallader to Gorton (Walk 4) *Photograph by Bob Sawers*

Gorton Bothy *(Walk 4)* *Photograph by Bill Goldie*

WALK 1

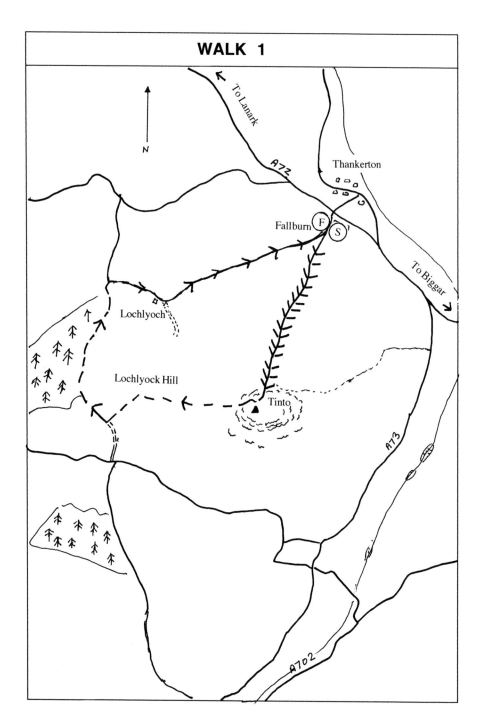

WALK 1

ROUTE	Tinto	ORD. SURVEY	72
DISTANCE	9 miles	GRADE	B+
COMFORT STOP	Biggar	SOCIAL STOP	Biggar
START WALK	Fallburn	GRID REF	965 375
FINISH WALK	Fallburn	GRID REF	965 375

DESCRIPTION

One of the most prominent hills in Lanarkshire, Tinto offers magnificent views over the surrounding area. The summit is quite unique, consisting of huge stones and boulders rising to the base of the trig. point. There are several stone windbreaks around the summit, offering welcome shelter on a cold windy day.

WALK DETAILS

Start the walk at the junction of the A73 and the minor road to Thankerton. Go past Fallburn and follow a well defined trail to the summit. Take a bearing to Lochlyock Hill and head down to Housegate Mouth, turning right towards Lochlyoch Farm, then continue to Fallburn.

METALLED ROAD	4 miles	LRT	
TRAIL	3 miles	NO TRAIL	2 miles
STARTING HEIGHT	600 ft.	MAXIMUM HEIGHT	2,301 ft.
HEIGHT CLIMBED	1,701 ft.		
BUS PICK-UP POINT	Fallburn		

WALK 2

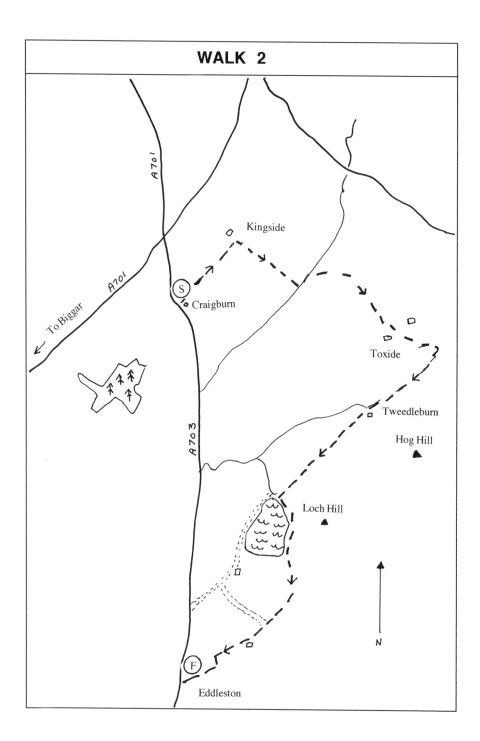

WALK 2

ROUTE	Craigburn to Eddleston	ORD. SURVEY	73
DISTANCE	10 miles	GRADE	C+
COMFORT STOP	Biggar	SOCIAL STOP	Biggar
START WALK	Craigburn	GRID REF	239 543
FINISH WALK	Eddleston	GRID REF	243 482

DESCRIPTION

This is an easy moorland walk. The route is in the foothills of the Moorfoots and round Portmore Loch. The loch is used for fishing. It is not permitted to go down the LRT past Portmore House.

WALK DETAILS

Begin at Craigburn on the A703. Follow the road to Kingside then on to Lockmuir then turn left to pick up LRT to Toxide and after about half a mile turn right to Tweedleburn. Take the trail to Portmore Loch and go down the east side of the loch past Loch Hill. Follow the trail to Boreland then on to Eddleston.

METALLED ROAD	3 miles	LRT	5 miles
TRAIL	2 miles	NO TRAIL	
STARTING HEIGHT	849 ft.	MAXIMUM HEIGHT	918 ft.
HEIGHT CLIMBED	79 ft.		
BUS PICK-UP POINT	A703 at Eddleston		

WALK 3

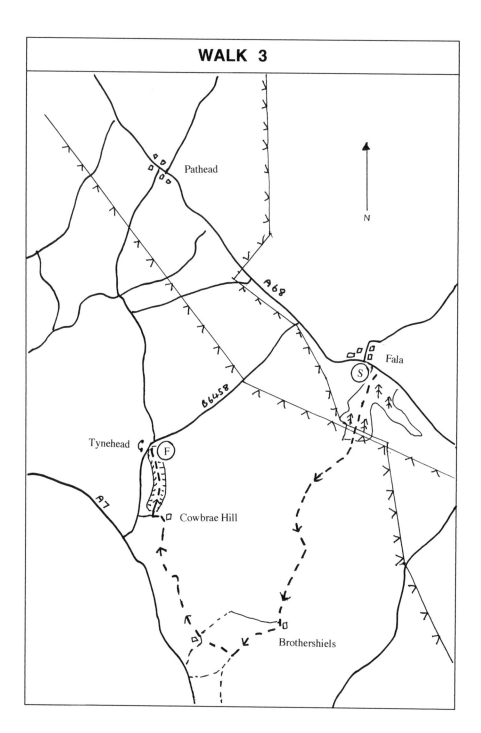

Pathead

N

A68

B6458

Fala

S

Tynehead

F

A7

Cowbrae Hill

Brothershiels

WALK 3

ROUTE	Fala to Tynehead	**ORD. SURVEY**	66
DISTANCE	8 miles	**GRADE**	C+
COMFORT STOP	Kirk o' Shott Services	**SOCIAL STOP**	Pathhead
START WALK	Fala	**GRID REF**	437 610
FINISH WALK	Tynehead	**GRID REF**	394 592

DESCRIPTION

This walk is a typical moorland walk, crossing Fala Moor, in pleasant open country, with extended views of the Moorfoot Hills.

WALK DETAILS

The walk begins at Fala. Take the unclassified road up through the trees and under the power pylons to emerge on an LRT leading to Brothershiels Farm. From here take the road to Nettingflat at which point turn right and contour across the hill to Cowbrae Hill to pick up the trail along the disused railway line to Tynehead.

METALLED ROAD	1 mile	**LRT**	6 miles
TRAIL	1 mile	**NO TRAIL**	
STARTING HEIGHT	690 ft.	**MAXIMUM HEIGHT**	996 ft.
HEIGHT CLIMBED	306 ft.		
BUS PICK-UP POINT	B6367 at Tynehead		

WALK 4

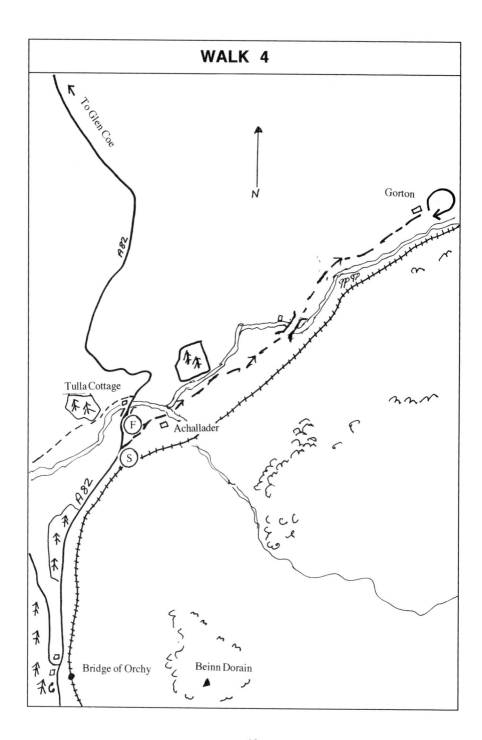

To Glen Coe

A82

N

Gorton

Tulla Cottage

F

S

Achallader

A82

Bridge of Orchy

Beinn Dorain

WALK 4

ROUTE	Achallader to Gorton	**ORD. SURVEY**	50
DISTANCE	10 miles	**GRADE**	C+
COMFORT STOP	Tyndrum	**SOCIAL STOP**	Ardlui
START WALK	Achallader	**GRID REF**	312 436
FINISH WALK	Achallader	**GRID REF**	312 436

DESCRIPTION

This walk is on LRT all the way to Gorton Bothy. Near the start of the walk a river has to be crossed, this is wide and shallow. The route goes between high mountain ranges and Gorton Bothy is a suitable place to stop and have something to eat and drink. The bothy is in quite good condition, and in wet weather will hold a large group.

WALK DETAILS

Take the LRT past Achallader Farm and wade the river at Allt Coire Achallader. One mile later cross the bridge at the Water of Tulla. Follow the LRT all the way to Gorton Bothy and return by the same route.

METALLED ROAD		**LRT**	10 miles
TRAIL		**NO TRAIL**	
STARTING HEIGHT	522 ft.	**MAXIMUM HEIGHT**	900 ft.
HEIGHT CLIMBED	378 ft.		
BUS PICK-UP POINT	Just off the A82 at Achallader Car Park		

Hermitage to Bee Cottage (Walk 5)   Photograph by Myra Sawers

Hermitage to Bee Cottage (Walk 5)   Photograph by Myra Sawers

Meikle Bin from Cort ma Law (Walk 6)   Photograph by Myra Sawers

Trig Point, Cort ma Law   (Walk 6)   Photograph by Myra Sawers

WALK 5

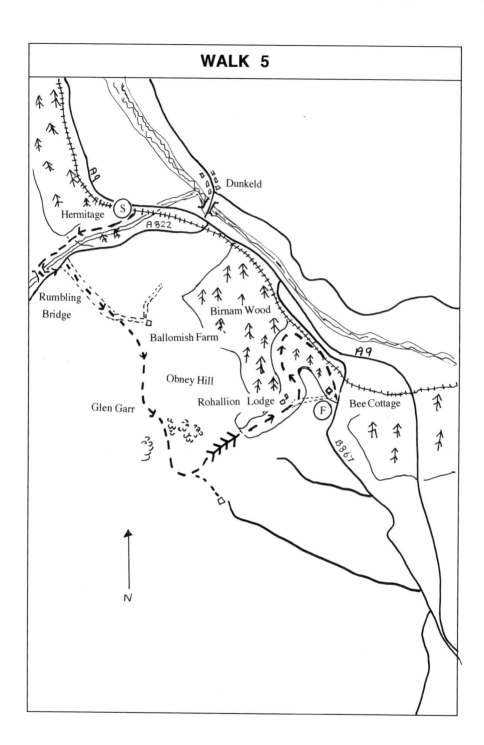

WALK 5

ROUTE	Hermitage to Bee Cottage	**ORD. SURVEY**	52
DISTANCE	9 miles	**GRADE**	C+
COMFORT STOP	Dunkeld	**SOCIAL STOP**	Dunkeld
START WALK	The Hermitage	**GRID REF**	999 423
FINISH WALK	Bee Cottage	**GRID REF**	052 392

DESCRIPTION

The Hermitage is a beautiful wooded area of some 37 acres, with spectacular views of the waterfall from the Hermitage viewpoint high above the River Braan. Experience the atmosphere at Rumbling Bridge before traversing beautiful Glen Garr on a high green path, finishing with a pleasant woodland walk.

WALK DETAILS

The walk begins at The Hermitage on the A9. Follow the trail to Rumbling Bridge, then turn left and take the LRT to Balhomish Farm. Just before the farm take the trail down Glen Garr, contouring round Obney Hill to map ref. 023 373. Cross open ground to pick up the LRT to Rohallian Lodge, then go round Birnam Wood to finish at Bee Cottage.

METALLED ROAD		**LRT**	5 miles
TRAIL	3 miles	**NO TRAIL**	1 mile
STARTING HEIGHT	150 ft.	**MAXIMUM HEIGHT**	750 ft.
HEIGHT CLIMBED	600 ft.		
BUS PICK-UP POINT	Bee Cottage on B867		

WALK 6

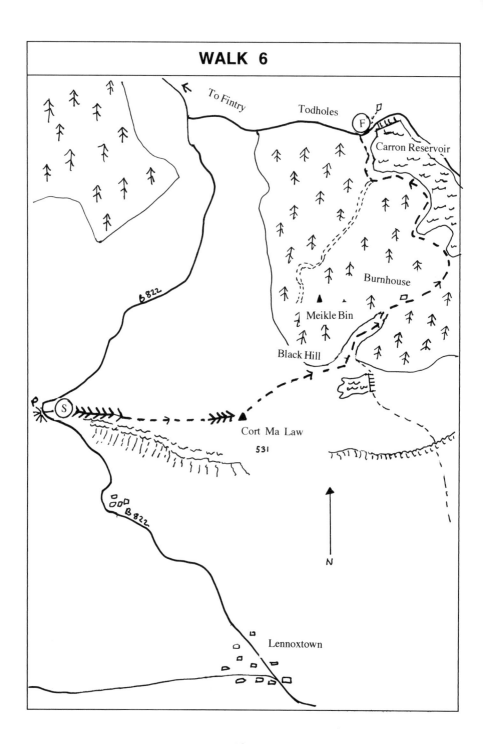

To Fintry
Todholes
F
Carron Reservoir
Burnhouse
Meikle Bin
Black Hill
B822
P
S
Cort Ma Law
531
B822
N
Lennoxtown

WALK 6

ROUTE	Cort ma Law to Todholes	ORD. SURVEY	64/57
DISTANCE	9 miles	GRADE	B
COMFORT STOP	Stirling Service Station	SOCIAL STOP	Fintry
START WALK	B822	GRID REF	612 801
FINISH WALK	Todholes	GRID REF	673 861

DESCRIPTION

Starting above Lennoxtown this is a high level flat ridge walk in the Campsie Fells to the summit of Cort ma Law followed by open hill walking to reach the Carron Valley Forest, then through the forest to Todholes Farm.

From the summit of Cort Ma Law the distinct shape of the Meikle Bin can be seen.

WALK DETAILS

From the car park on the Crow Road (B822) take the trail up to the Cort ma Law summit. From there taking a bearing on grid 651 800 to 651 805 and take a bearing to the fire break at Black Hill. Follow the LRT to the ruins of Burnhouse, and walk out on the LRT to Todholes.

METALLED ROAD		LRT	4 miles
TRAIL	3 miles	NO TRAIL	2 miles
STARTING HEIGHT	750 ft.	MAXIMUM HEIGHT	1,563 ft.
HEIGHT CLIMBED	813 ft.		
BUS PICK·UP POINT	Todholes Farm		

WALK 7

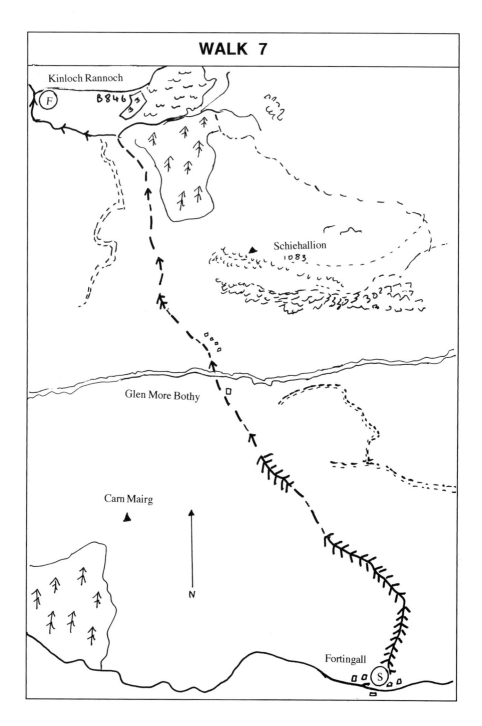

Kinloch Rannoch

B846

Schiehallion
1083

Glen More Bothy

Carn Mairg

N

Fortingall

S

WALK 7

ROUTE	Fortingall to Kinloch Rannoch	ORD. SURVEY	51
DISTANCE	10 miles	GRADE	B+
COMFORT STOP	Aberfeldy	SOCIAL STOP	Dunkeld
START WALK	Fortingall	GRID REF	735 472
FINISH WALK	Kinloch Rannoch	GRID REF	662 587

DESCRIPTION

The start of this walk is fairly steep but the LRT takes the walker up easily to the maximum height. The views are magnificent and in particular the view of Schiehallion. The walk finishes on a pleasant downhill LRT to the road to Kinloch Rannoch.

WALK DETAILS

Start just past driveway to Glen Lyon House, where an LRT leads past some houses, to link with the LRT to Glenmore Bothy. This bothy is in good condition, but is quite difficult to spot, look out for the chimney above the mound on your right. Take a bearing to the LRT at 699 546, cross the river and head for Lassintullich.

METALLED ROAD	2 miles	LRT	6 miles
TRAIL		NO TRAIL	2 miles
STARTING HEIGHT	369 ft.	MAXIMUM HEIGHT	2,100 ft.
HEIGHT CLIMBED	1,731 ft.		
BUS PICK-UP POINT	Kinloch Rannoch Square		

Fortingall to Kinloch Rannoch (Walk 7)   Photograph by Billy Boyd

Glen More Bothy   *(Walk 7)*   Photograph by Billy Boyd

Findhu Glen to Comrie (Walk 8)   Photograph by Billy Boyd

Findhu Glen to Comrie (Walk 8)   Photograph by Billy Boyd

WALK 8

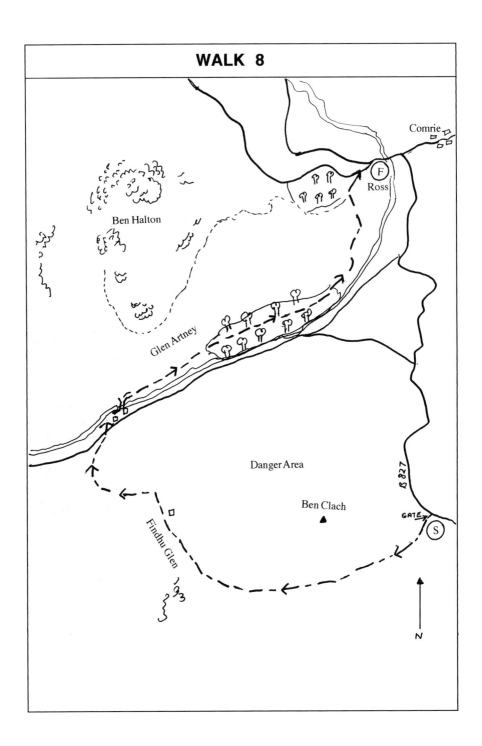

Comrie

F
Ross

Ben Halton

Glen Artney

Danger Area

Ben Clach ▲

B 827

GATE

S

Findhu Glen

N

WALK 8

ROUTE	Findhu Glen to Comrie	ORD. SURVEY	57
DISTANCE	11 miles	GRADE	B
COMFORT STOP	Crieff	SOCIAL STOP	Comrie
START WALK	Findhu Glen	GRID REF	780 151
FINISH WALK	Comrie	GRID REF	771 222

DESCRIPTION

This surely must be one of the most rewarding walks in Perthshire, going over open moorland and through Findhu Glen following the river, then crossing into Glen Artney, with a magnificent river walk, a woodland section and some green path, finishing at Comrie.

WALK DETAILS

Start on B827. As you pass Langside watch for a small building on your right, map ref. 788 149, then look for a gate on your left, at map ref. 780 151. Go through this gate and follow the path to join the LRT at the Corriebeagh Burn. Do not cross the bridge, but follow the LRT all the way to the minor road at Glen Artney. Turn right here and go down past Dalchruin. Cross the river and follow the LRT to Comrie.

METALLED ROAD	2 miles	LRT	6 miles
TRAIL	3 miles	NO TRAIL	
STARTING HEIGHT	672 ft.	MAXIMUM HEIGHT	750 ft.
HEIGHT CLIMBED	78 ft.		
BUS PICK-UP POINT	Car Park at Comrie.		

WALK 9

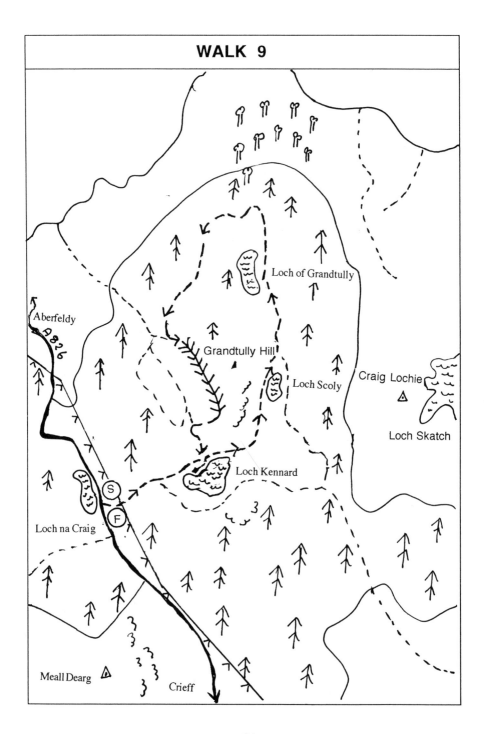

Loch of Grandtully

Aberfeldy

A826

Grandtully Hill

Loch Scoly

Craig Lochie

Loch Skatch

Loch Kennard

Loch na Craig

S

F

Meall Dearg

Crieff

WALK 9

ROUTE	Loch na Craig (Circular)	**ORD. SURVEY**	52
DISTANCE	10 miles	**GRADE**	C+
COMFORT STOP	Crieff	**SOCIAL STOP**	Dunkeld
START WALK	Loch na Craig	**GRID REF**	885 452
FINISH WALK	Loch na Craig	**GRID REF**	885 452

DESCRIPTION

Although this walk appears to be through the forest, the LRT is clear of the trees, and superb views are seen along the 10 mile route. A stop at the fisherman's hut on Loch Kennard is a must. There are three lochs on the route to be enjoyed, and as you leave Loch of Grantully there are unrestricted views of Aberfeldy and Schehallian.

WALK DETAILS

Start at the LRT opposite Loch na Craig and follow the route past Loch Kennard, Loch Scoly and Loch of Grantully. Circle round Grantully Hill to rejoin the outward route at Loch Kennard and return to Loch na Craig.

METALLED ROAD	**LRT**	10 miles
TRAIL	**NO TRAIL**	
STARTING HEIGHT 1,193 ft.	**MAXIMUM HEIGHT** 1,500 ft.	
HEIGHT CLIMBED 307 ft.		
BUS PICK-UP POINT Loch na Craig on A826.		

WALK 10

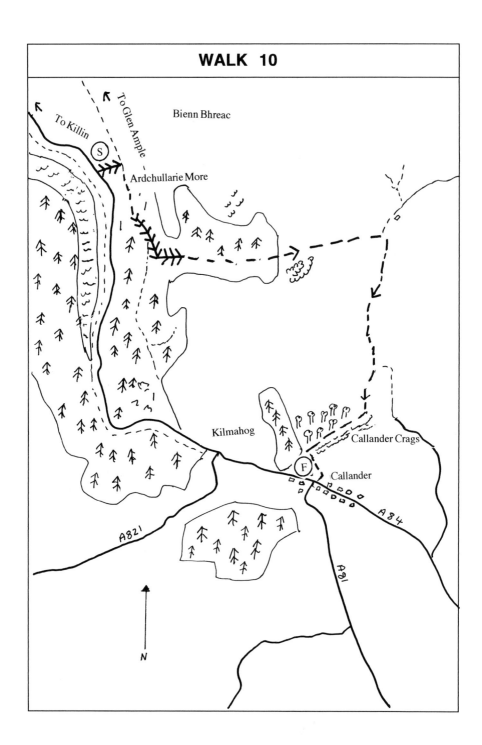

WALK 10

ROUTE	Loch Lubnaig to Callander	**ORD. SURVEY**	57
DISTANCE	9 miles	**GRADE**	B
COMFORT STOP	Callander	**SOCIAL STOP**	Callander
START WALK	Ardchullarie More	**GRID REF**	582 137
FINISH WALK	Callander	**GRID REF**	635 075

DESCRIPTION

A steep hill walk up through the forest to emerge high above Loch Lubnaig, and then over open moorland to finish at the Callander Crags. The countryside here is very scenic and this is a walk well worth doing.

WALK DETAILS

From Ardchullarie More on the A84 (this is the same start as for Glen Ample) climb through the trees and turn right at the junction where the trail joins an LRT. Follow this LRT to high open ground, then cross the open moorland. There is a deer fence which has to be climbed at this point. Take the LRT towards the Callander Crags, and follow the trail down to the car park.

METALLED ROAD	2 miles	**LRT**	4 miles
TRAIL	1 mile	**NO TRAIL**	2 miles
STARTING HEIGHT	387 ft.	**MAXIMUM HEIGHT**	1,350 ft.
HEIGHT CLIMBED	963 ft.		
BUS PICK-UP POINT	Car Park at Callander		

WALK 11

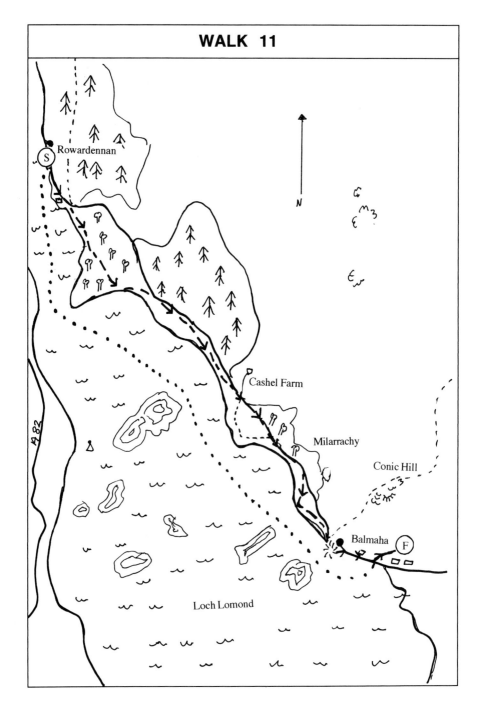

Rowardennan

Cashel Farm

Milarrachy

Conic Hill

Balmaha

Loch Lomond

A82

WALK 11

ROUTE	Rowardennan to Balmaha	ORD. SURVEY	56
DISTANCE	9 miles	GRADE	C+
COMFORT STOP	Drymen	SOCIAL STOP	Drymen
START WALK	Rowardennan	GRID REF	359 987
FINISH WALK	Balmaha	GRID REF	419 909

DESCRIPTION

A walk with everything .... a bus trip, a boat trip and a walk! The route from
Rowardennan follows the side of Loch Lomond and has spectacular views of one
of Scotland's best loved lochs. Choose your lunch spot to get the best views of the
loch. Part of the walk is along the shore of the loch, and part is in beautiful
deciduous forest.

WALK DETAILS

Book your boat trip from Macfarlane's Boatyard at Balmaha, sail to Rowardennan
and then follow the West Highland Way trail which as often as possible follows the
shoreline of Loch Lomond, to finish at Balmaha.

METALLED ROAD	2 miles	LRT	
TRAIL	7 miles	NO TRAIL	
STARTING HEIGHT	66 ft.	MAXIMUM HEIGHT	252 ft.
HEIGHT CLIMBED	186 ft.		
BUS PICK-UP POINT	Balmaha Car Park		

Loch Lubnaig to Callander (Walk 10)   Photograph by Mike Callaghan

Loch Lubnaig to Callander (Walk 10)   Photograph by Mike Callaghan

Rowardennan to Balmaha (Walk 11)   Photograph by Bob Sawers

Rowardennan to Balmaha (Walk 11)   Photograph by Bob Sawers

WALK12

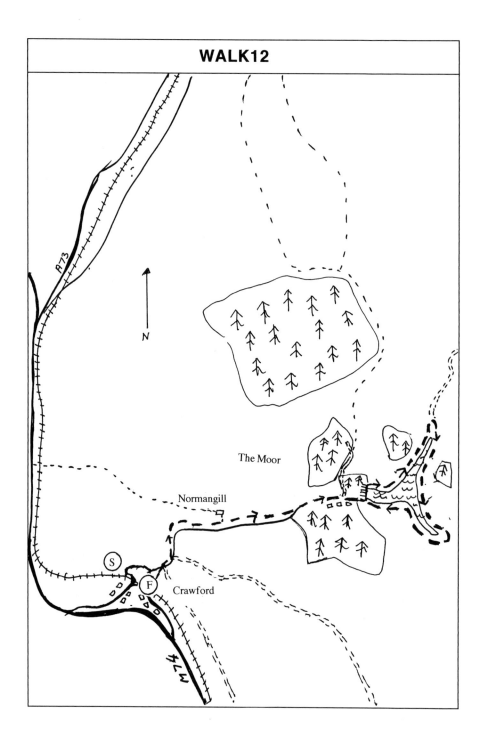

A73

N

The Moor

Normangill

S

F   Crawford

M74

42

WALK 12

ROUTE	Camps Reservoir	**ORD. SURVEY**	72
DISTANCE	11 miles	**GRADE**	C
COMFORT STOP	Abington Service Centre	**SOCIAL STOP**	Crawford
START WALK	Crawford	**GRID REF**	956 210
FINISH WALK	Crawford	**GRID REF**	956 210

DESCRIPTION

A pleasant walk on a green trail, with unobstructed views of the hills surrounding Camps Reservoir. The route offers continually changing views surrounding this unusually shaped reservoir. There are usually fishermen to be seen around the reservoir. Prior to walking contact should be made with the resident Water Engineer. (tel: 018642 210).

WALK DETAILS

The walk begins at the post office and church in Crawford. Take the footpath down and across the railway bridge, then pick up the disused railway line to Midlock at the road junction. After Midlock move to the left and you will find a green path running parallel with the road all the way to the dam. Cross the dam, and go around the reservoir in a clockwise direction. As you approach the dam for a second time go down the trail through the woods, then return by the same route.

METALLED ROAD		**LRT**	5 miles
TRAIL	6 miles	**NO TRAIL**	
STARTING HEIGHT	700 ft.	**MAXIMUM HEIGHT**	900 ft.
HEIGHT CLIMBED	200 ft.		
BUS PICK-UP POINT	Main Street, Crawford, where the walk started.		

WALK 13

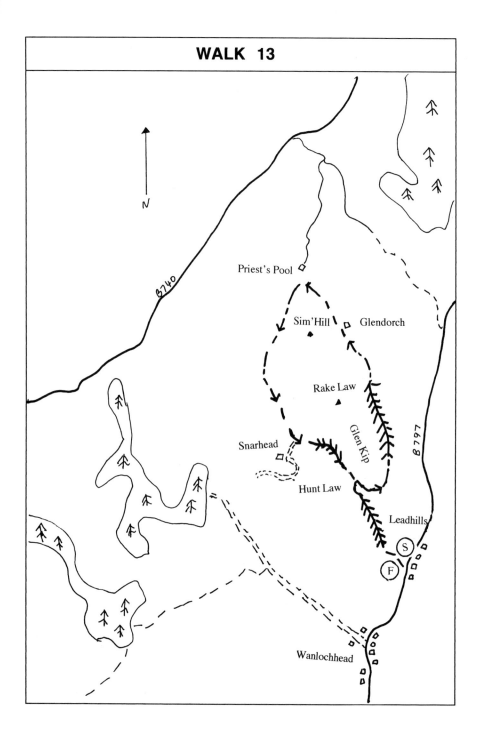

Priest's Pool

Sim'Hill   Glendorch

Rake Law

Glen Kip

Snarhead

Hunt Law

Leadhills

S

F

Wanlochhead

B740

B797

N

WALK 13

ROUTE	Leadhills	ORD. SURVEY	78
DISTANCE	9 miles	GRADE	C+
COMFORT STOP	Abington Service Centre	SOCIAL STOP	Crawford
START WALK	Leadhills	GRID REF	884 144
FINISH WALK	Leadhills	GRID REF	884 144

DESCRIPTION

This walk is full of surprising views of the horseshoe curve overlooking Glen Kip. The LRT changes to a grass trail as it heads towards Glendorch (ruin), which is a good lunch spot. Route is on open hill and conditions underfoot are good. Lowther Hill and Green Lowther can be seen from the top of Hunt Law, both of them have radar stations.

WALK DETAILS

Start on the LRT up Hunt Law. Turn right at the junction and go round to Glendorch (this is a ruin). Make a decision on whether to go down to the Priest's Pool or keep on a high contour route leading round to Snarhead. Take the LRT up Hunt Law, then down to the B797.

METALLED ROAD		LRT	5 miles
TRAIL	4 miles	NO TRAIL	
STARTING HEIGHT	1,200 ft.	MAXIMUM HEIGHT	1,602 ft.
HEIGHT CLIMBED	402 ft.		
BUS PICK-UP POINT	Leadhills (at drop off spot).		

WALK 14

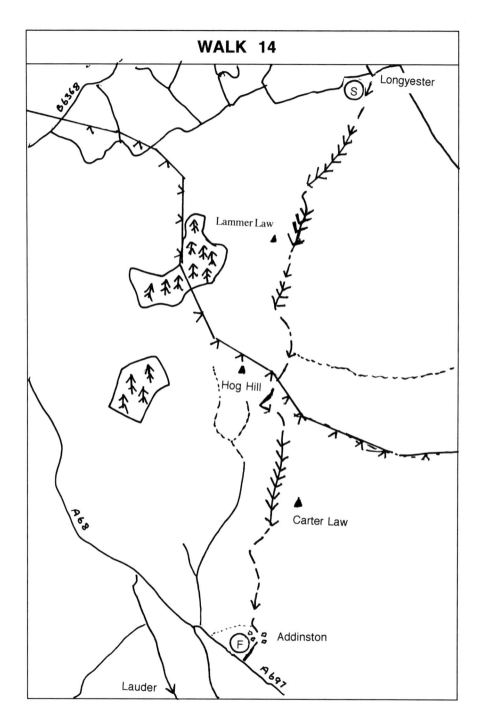

Longyester

Lammer Law

Hog Hill

Carter Law

Addinston

Lauder

WALK 14

ROUTE	Gifford to Addington	ORD. SURVEY	66
DISTANCE	8miles	GRADE	B
COMFORT STOP	Gifford	SOCIAL STOP	Pathhead
START WALK	Gifford	GRID REF	531 677
FINISH WALK	Addington	GRID REF	518 527

DESCRIPTION

This is a good high level ridge walk through the Lammermoor hills starting at the village of Gifford, which is very pretty and well worth a visit, and finishing at the hamlet of Addington.

WALK DETAILS

Leave Gifford on the B6355, and after a short distance take the minor road leading to Yester Mains Farm. Carry on to Long Yester, passing Blinkbonny Wood, and on to an LRT to Tollishill. Take the trail up the hill to the ruin, then continue past Addington Hill to finish at Addington.

METALLED ROAD		LRT	4 miles
TRAIL	4 miles	NO TRAIL	
STARTING HEIGHT	402 ft.	MAXIMUM HEIGHT	1.500 ft.
HEIGHT CLIMBED	1,098 ft.		
BUS PICK-UP POINT	A697 at Addington		

WALK 15

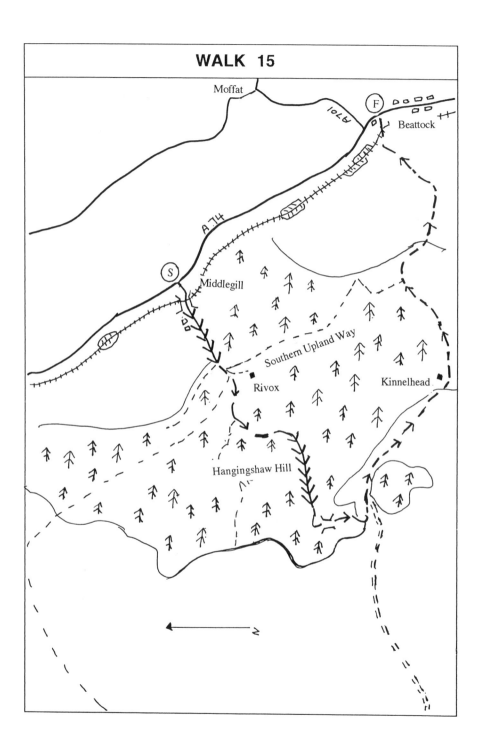

Moffat

Beattock

A701

A74

Middlegill

S

Southern Upland Way

Rivox

Kinnelhead

Hangingshaw Hill

F

WALK 15

ROUTE	Middlegill to Beattock	ORD. SURVEY	78
DISTANCE	10 miles	GRADE	B
COMFORT STOP	Moffat	SOCIAL STOP	Moffat
START WALK	Middlegill	GRID REF	048 068
FINISH WALK	Beattock	GRID REF	078 028

DESCRIPTION

This is in the main a forest walk, and it takes in part of the Southern Upland Way near the Daer Reservoir. The route opens out into a narrow valley and follows the river for a short spell before turning through woodland again to emerge at Beattock.

WALK DETAILS

Start at Middlegill on the (M)A74. Go under the railway and then take the LRT to the junction before Rivox. Take the right fork and at the next junction turn left and contour around Hangingshaw Hill. Follow the LRT to Blairmack and then on to Kinnelhead. Cross the river and walk out to Beattock.

METALLED ROAD	3 miles	LRT	7 miles
TRAIL		NO TRAIL	
STARTING HEIGHT	300 ft.	MAXIMUM HEIGHT	1,200 ft.
HEIGHT CLIMBED	900 ft.		
BUS PICK-UP POINT	Beattock		

Camps Reservoir (Walk 12)   Photograph by Mike Callaghan

Camps Reservoir (Walk 12)   Photograph by Mike Callaghan

Glen Ogle Cottage (Walk 17)　　　　　　*Photograph by Mike Callaghan*

Glen Ogle Cottage (Walk 17)　　　　　　*Photograph by Billy Boyd*

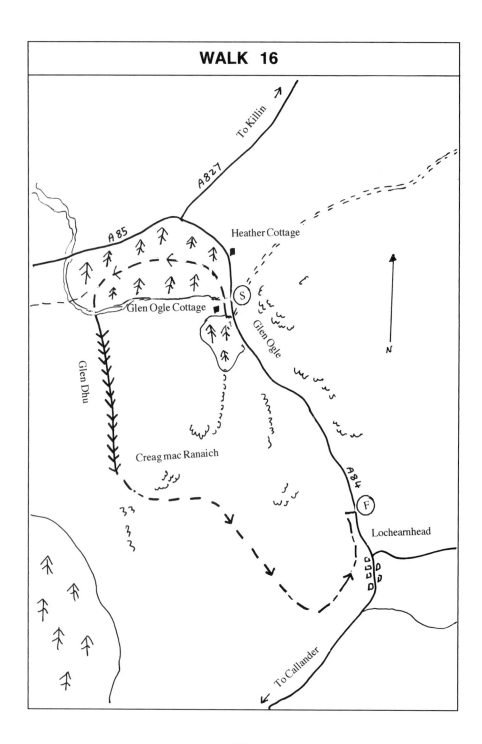

WALK 16

ROUTE	Glen Ogle Cottage	ORD. SURVEY 51	
DISTANCE	9 miles	**GRADE**	B+
COMFORT STOP	Callander	**SOCIAL STOP**	Callander
START WALK	Glen Ogle Cottage	**GRID REF** 555 264	
FINISH WALK	Loch Earnhead	**GRID REF** 589 240	

DESCRIPTION

This walk begins by a walk through a forest then climbs steadily up Glean Dubh with fine open views of the surrounding hills. From the summit there are panoramic views of Ben Vorlich and Stuc a Chroin and from the disused railway line an unrestricted view of Loch Earn.

WALK DETAILS

From the car park go down the side of Glen Ogle Cottage to join the disused railway line. Follow this to the remains of the old platform at Glendhu. Look out for an LRT on the left leading up Gleann Dubh. Ford the river, and follow the LRT all the way to join the disused railway line. Leave trail at path to the Scout Hut.

METALLED ROAD		LRT	9 miles
TRAIL		**NO TRAIL**	
STARTING HEIGHT	600 ft.	**MAXIMUM HEIGHT**	1,950 ft.
HEIGHT CLIMBED	1,350 ft.		
BUS PICK-UP POINT	Car park at Lochearnhead		

WALK 17

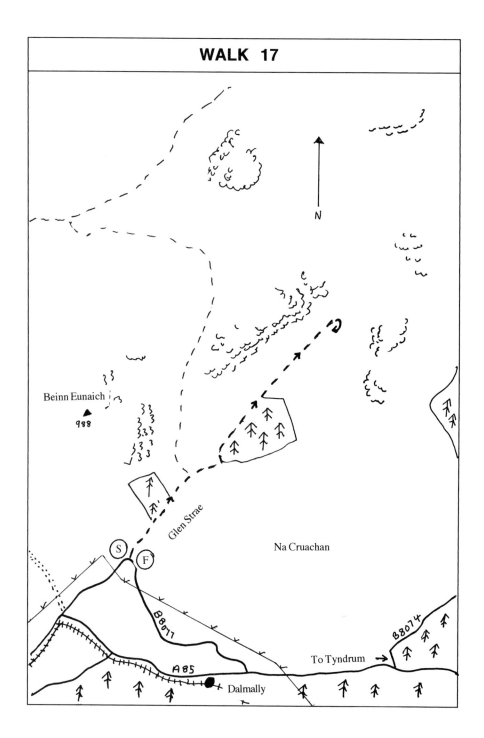

N

Beinn Eunaich
988

Glen Strae

S F

Na Cruachan

B8077

B8074

To Tyndrum →

A85

Dalmally

WALK 17

ROUTE	Glen Strae	**ORD. SURVEY**	50
DISTANCE	10 miles	**GRADE**	C+
COMFORT STOP	Tyndrum	**SOCIAL STOP**	Ardlui
START WALK	Glen Strae	**GRID REF**	145 295
FINISH WALK	Glen Strae	**GRID REF**	145 295

DESCRIPTION

This route goes through Glen Strae with high mountain ridges on each side. Watch out for buzzards or even on the rare occasion eagles soaring overhead. The LRT follows close to the river and there are many pleasant riverside lunch spots.

WALK DETAILS

Start on the B8077 just past the monument (worth a look).

Follow the LRT all the way till it ends at the river, then return by the same route.

METALLED ROAD	**LRT**	10 miles
TRAIL	**NO TRAIL**	
STARTING HEIGHT 156 ft.	**MAXIMUM HEIGHT**	300 ft.
HEIGHT CLIMBED 244 ft.		
BUS PICK UP POINT Glen Strae		

WALK 18

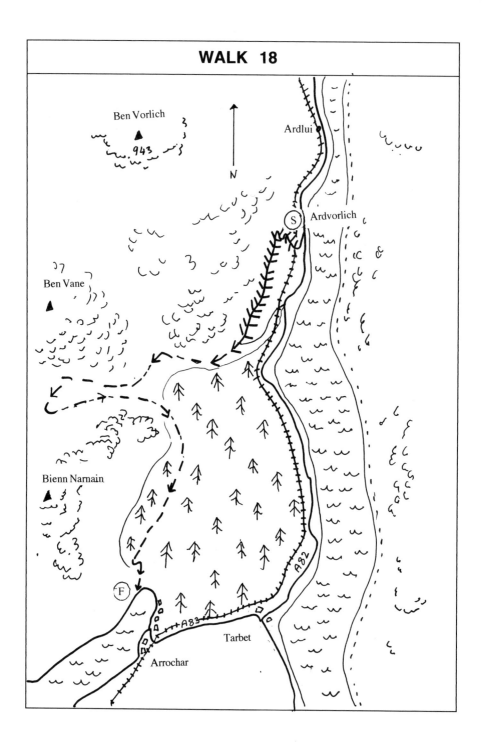

WALK 18

ROUTE	Advorlich to Arrochar	**ORD. SURVEY** 56	
DISTANCE	9 miles	**GRADE**	B
COMFORT STOP	Arrochar	**SOCIAL STOP**	Arrochar
START WALK	Advorlich	**GRID REF**	325 121
FINISH WALK	Succoth	**GRID REF**	295 050

DESCRIPTION

The steep climb at the start of the walk affords unrestricted views of Loch Lomond and the surrounding hills, Ben a Choin, Stob an Fhainne and of course the wonderful sight of Ben Lomond. This high level route contours around Ben Vorlich and drops down to Inverruglas Water, finishing with an interesting forest walk round to Succoth.

WALK DETAILS

Keep a sharp lookout for the start on the A82. Advorlich is a cottage with a barn at the side. Go through the gate and immediately turn left. The LRT goes under the railway and winds its way up the hill. Continue round to the junction of LRTs above Succoth and either go round the LRT or watch out for the trail down by the burn to Succoth.

METALLED ROAD	**LRT**	9 miles
TRAIL	**NO TRAIL**	
STARTING HEIGHT 36 ft.	**MAXIMUM HEIGHT** 900 ft.	
HEIGHT CLIMBED 864 ft.		
BUS PICK-UP POINT Lay-by at Succoth or car park, Arrochar.		

WALK 19

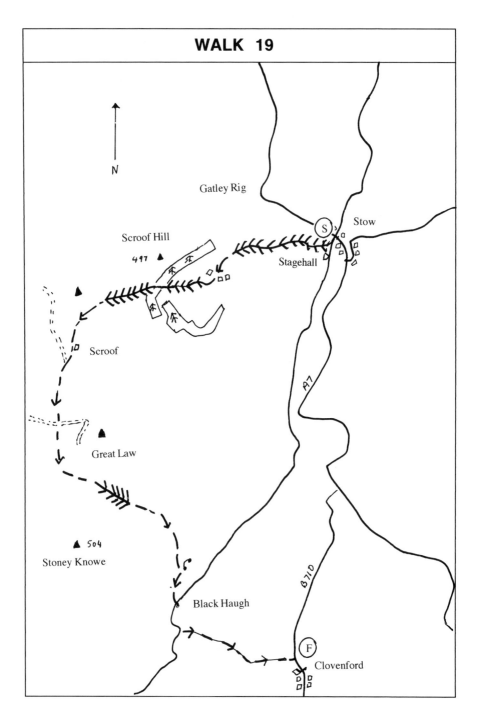

WALK 19

ROUTE	Stagehall to Clovenford	ORD. SURVEY	73
DISTANCE	10 miles	GRADE	B
COMFORT STOP	Lauder	SOCIAL STOP	Pathhead
START WALK	Stagehall	GRID REF	454 444
FINISH WALK	Clovenford	GRID REF	449 363

DESCRIPTION

This walk has an easy start on a green trail and keeps high on the open heather-covered hills with long views towards Peebles. The ruined cottage at Scroof makes a good lunch spot. The walk from there is on an LRT alongside the Cadden Water and onwards to Cloverford.

WALK DETAILS

Start on the LRT by Stagehall Farm and go over Stagehall Hill. Cross Lugate Water to pick up the LRT to the Lodge. Cross Back Burn and head for the cairn (walking on the heather). Drop down steeply to Scroof, then follow the LRT to Blackhaugh and finish on a metalled road to Clovenford.

METALLED ROAD	2 miles	LRT	4 miles
TRAIL	4 miles	NO TRAIL	
STARTING HEIGHT	540 ft.	MAXIMUM HEIGHT	1,350 ft.
HEIGHT CLIMBED	810 ft.		
BUS PICK-UP POINT	Clovenford		

Advorlich to Arrochar (Walk 18)   *Photograph by Myra Sawers*

Advorlich to Arrochar (Walk 18)   *Photograph by Myra Sawers*

Loch na Craig (Walk 9)   Photograph by Myra Sawers

Loch na Craig (Walk 9)   Photograph by Myra Sawers

WALK 20

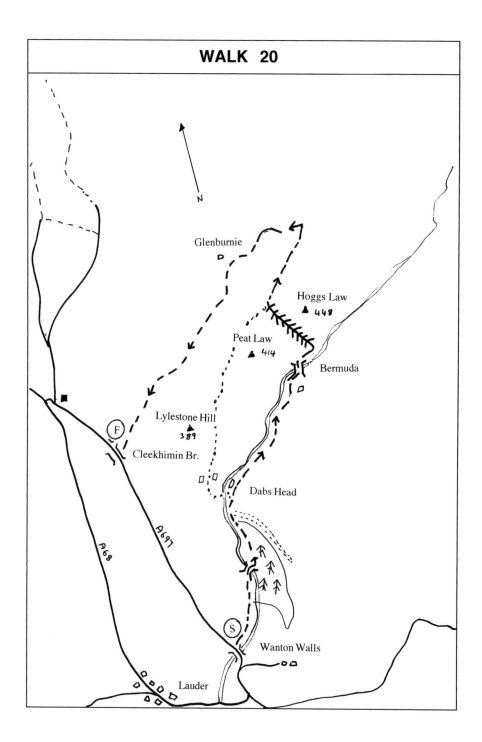

Glenburnie

Hoggs Law
▲ 448

Peat Law
▲ 414

Bermuda

Lylestone Hill
▲
389

Cleekhimin Br.

Dabs Head

A691

A68

F

S

Wanton Walls

Lauder

WALK 20

ROUTE	Wanton Walls to Cleekhimin	ORD. SURVEY	73
DISTANCE	10 miles	GRADE	B
COMFORT STOP	Lauder	SOCIAL STOP	Pathhead
START WALK	River at Wanton Walls	GRID REF	543 487
FINISH WALK	Cleekhimin Bridge	GRID REF	522 523

DESCRIPTION

This starts with an interesting river walk to Bermuda, then progresses up over heather-covered hills into a valley, with an alternative high level but very safe hill walk.

WALK DETAILS

Start where the A697 crosses the River Earnscleugh. Keep to the low LRT next to the river. At the end of this LRT cross the grass area to pick up the LRT coming downhill. Here you can turn left to Burncastle and follow the ridge all the way to Wedderlaw, or keep going on this LRT to Bermuda, crossing the bridge and heading for the cairn. From the cairn strike out for Wedderlaw and pick up the LRT at Glenburnie.

METALLED ROAD	1 mile	LRT	6 miles
TRAIL	3 miles	NO TRAIL	
STARTING HEIGHT	567 ft.	MAXIMUM HEIGHT	1,200 ft.
HEIGHT CLIMBED	633 ft.		
BUS PICK-UP POINT	Cleekhimin Bridge		

WALK 21

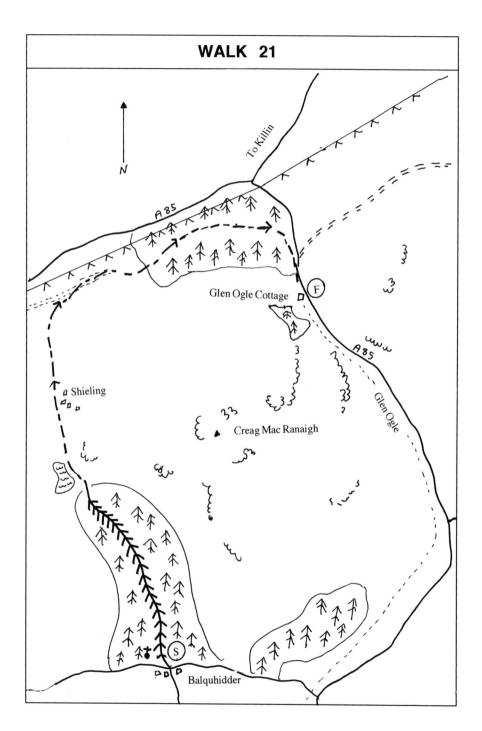

N

To Killin

A85

Glen Ogle Cottage

F

A85

Glen Ogle

Shieling

Creag Mac Ranaigh

S

Balquhidder

WALK 21

ROUTE	Balquidder to Glen Ogle	ORD. SURVEY 51	
DISTANCE	8 miles	GRADE	B+
COMFORT STOP	Callander	SOCIAL STOP	Callander
START WALK	Balquidder	GRID REF	535 199
FINISH WALK	Glen Ogle Cottage	GRID REF	559 284

DESCRIPTION

From Balquidder Church, where time can be taken to see the grave of Rob Roy MacGregor, the walk up through the forest is very pleasant and emerges on to open hills near Lochan an Eireannaich, look for a good lunch spot here. Follow the high trail over to the shielings, affording distant views of Glen Dochart.

WALK DETAILS

Start at Balquidder Church and take the LRT up Kirkton Glen which merges with an open trail to Lochan an Eireannaich. Take the high trail just below Meall an Fhiodhain, gradually dropping down to the shielings. Climb on to the viaduct and follow the bed of the disused railway track to Glen Ogle Cottage.

METALLED ROAD		LRT	
TRAIL		NO TRAIL	
STARTING HEIGHT	396 ft.	MAXIMUM HEIGHT	2,100 ft.
HEIGHT CLIMBED	1,704 ft.		
BUS PICK-UP POINT	Glen Ogle Cottage (car park)		

WALK 22

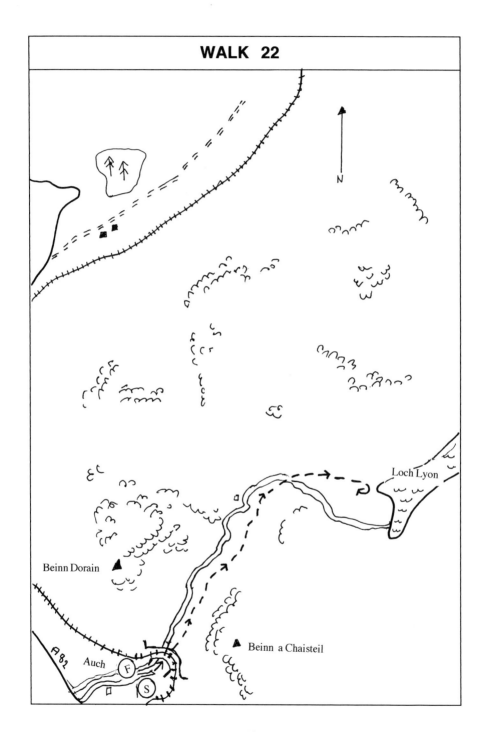

Loch Lyon

Beinn Dorain ▲

Beinn a Chaisteil ▲

Auch Ⓕ Ⓢ

A82

66

WALK 22

ROUTE	Auch	ORD. SURVEY	50
DISTANCE	10 miles	GRADE	C
COMFORT STOP	Tyndrum	SOCIAL STOP	Ardlui
START WALK	Auch	GRID REF	316 354
FINISH WALK	Auch	GRID REF	316 354

DESCRIPTION

Here is a level walk amongst the high hills. Look to Beinn Dorian on one side and Beinn a Chaisteil on the other, with a river walk thrown in for good measure. The views improve as you move further down Auch Gleann.

WALK DETAILS

Start at the road end on the A82. It should be noted that permission should be sought from Auch Farm, so that it is possible to take the bus down to the bridge. Go under the viaduct and cross the Allt Coralan River by wading. Although the LRT crosses the river Allt Kinglass further on, do not cross, but follow the trail which eventually links up with the LRT. There is another river to be crossed just before Strath Tarabhan. Return by the same route.

METALLED ROAD		LRT	
TRAIL		NO TRAIL	
STARTING HEIGHT	215 ft.	MAXIMUM HEIGHT	215 ft.
HEIGHT CLIMBED			
BUS PICK-UP POINT	Auch		

WALK 23

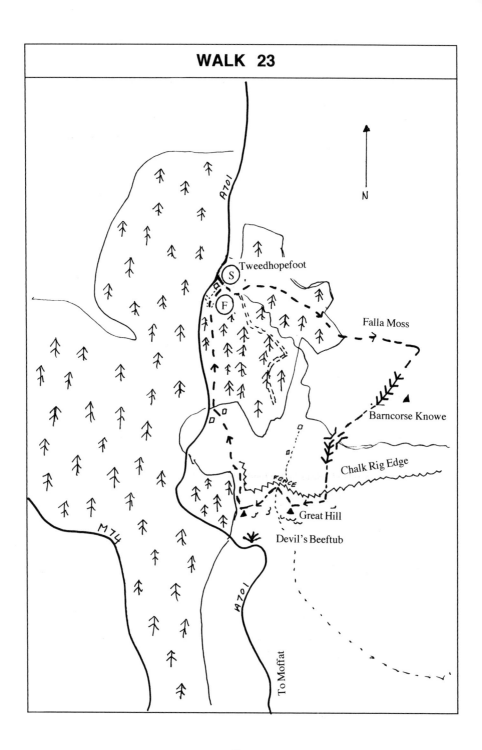

N

Tweedhopefoot

S

F

Falla Moss

Barncorse Knowe

Chalk Rig Edge

FENCE

Great Hill

Devil's Beeftub

M74

A701

A701

To Moffat

68

WALK 23

ROUTE	Devil's Beef Tub	ORD. SURVEY	78
DISTANCE	9 miles	GRADE	B
COMFORT STOP	Moffat	SOCIAL STOP	Moffat
START WALK	Tweedhopefoot	GRID REF	053 177
FINISH WALK	Tweedhopefoot	GRID REF	053 177

DESCRIPTION

Visit the smallest school in Scotland on this walk, and enjoy an interesting walk through forests and over open moorland. This walk is quite exposed in parts, although after viewing the Devil's Beef Tub the route quickly drops down to a more sheltered LRT.

WALK DETAILS

Start on the A701 8 miles from Moffat at Tweedhopefoot. Follow LRT through the forest heading for Glencragie Burn. At the end of the LRT go through the gate and contour below the summit of Falla Moss. Take a bearing to GR 085 165, then another bearing to the Crown of Scotland. Head for the footbridge over the Powskein Burn, and go over the Craigs to Chalk Rig Edge. At this point follow the wall to Great Hill then to the trig. point on Annanhead Hill. Go through the gate and follow the forest to meet an LRT leading to a farm. Go through the gate at the side of the barn and along the firebreak.

METALLED ROAD		LRT	3 miles
TRAIL	2 miles	NO TRAIL	4 miles
STARTING HEIGHT	1,025 ft.	MAXIMUM HEIGHT	1,644 ft.
HEIGHT CLIMBED	619 ft.		
BUS PICK-UP POINT	Tweedhopefoot on A70		

Devil's Beef Tub (Walk 23)   Photograph by Billy Boyd

Devil's Beef Tub (Walk 23)   Photograph by Billy Boyd

Taynuilt to Inverliver Bay (Walk 24) *Photograph by Myra Sawers*

Taynuilt to Inverliver Bay (Walk 24) *Photograph by Myra Sawers*

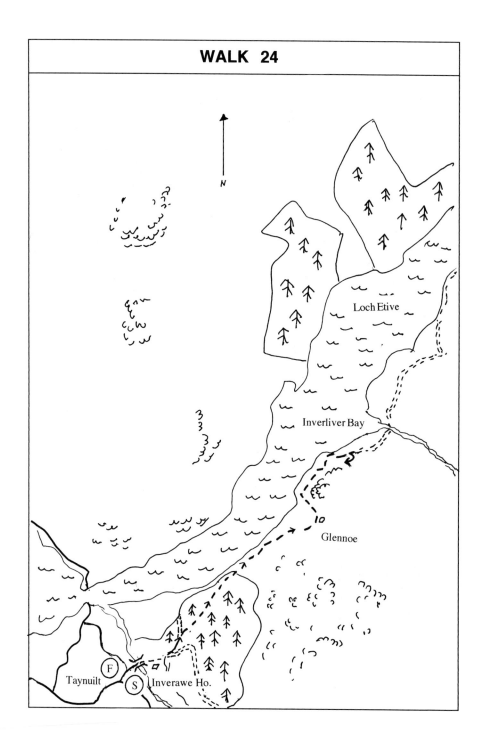

N

Loch Etive

Inverliver Bay

Glennoe

Taynuilt (F) (S) Inverawe Ho.

WALK 24

ROUTE	Taynuilt to Inverliver Bay	**ORD. SURVEY**	50
DISTANCE	10 miles	**GRADE**	C+
COMFORT STOP	Tyndrum	**SOCIAL STOP**	Ardlui
START WALK	Taynuilt	**GRID REF**	016 313
FINISH WALK	Taynuilt	**GRID REF**	016 313

DESCRIPTION

This walk is full of surprises! There is an interesting crossing of a suspension bridge, a look at a fish farm, a forest section and a lochside section. Some magnificient views from the high points looking down on Loch Etive. Nice lunch spot at Stron nam Feanag.

WALK DETAILS

From the bridge on the A85 just outside Taynuilt go down the LRT for a short distance and go through the gate on the right which leads to a suspension bridge. Pass Inverawe House and go up past the fishing pools, following the trail until the road is reached. From here go up the LRT. At the second junction (the first junction is not marked on the map) take the right fork and go all the way to Stron nam Feanag, overlooking Inverliver Bay. Return from this point.

METALLED ROAD	**LRT**	10 miles
TRAIL	**NO TRAIL**	
STARTING HEIGHT 71 ft.	**MAXIMUM HEIGHT**	300 ft.
HEIGHT CLIMBED 229 ft.		
BUS PICK-UP POINT Taynuilt at drop-off point		

WALK 25

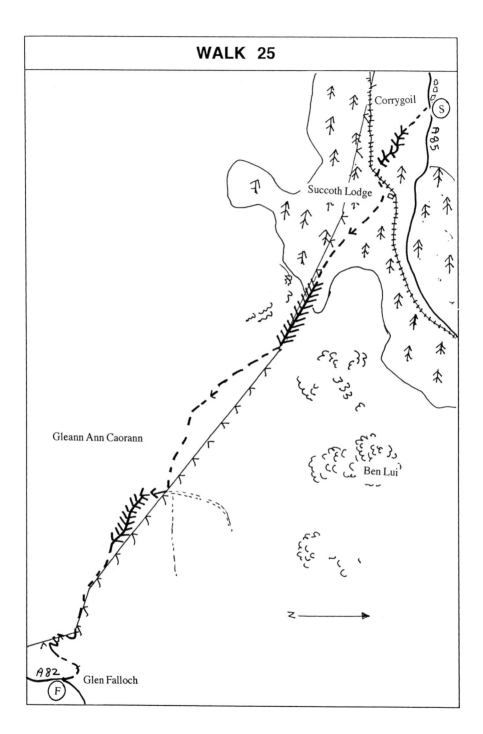

Corrygoil

S

A85

Succoth Lodge

Gleann Ann Caorann

Ben Lui

N

A82

Glen Falloch

F

WALK 25

ROUTE	Corrygoil to Glen Falloch	**ORD. SURVEY**	50
DISTANCE	10 miles	**GRADE**	B
COMFORT STOP	Tyndrum	**SOCIAL STOP**	Ardlui
START WALK	Corrygoyle	**GRID REF**	193 276
FINISH WALK	Glen Falloch	**GRID REF**	319 196

DESCRIPTION

Pleasant walk through forest and open moorland. This is deer country, so keep your eyes peeled. Unique views of Loch Lomond and surrounding hills on the approach to Glen Falloch.

WALK DETAILS

Start on the LRT opposite Corrygoil on the A85. Follow the LRT through the forest and then cross open moorland, taking a line roughly beside the pylon route and link up with the LRT next to the pipeline. From here it is a straight walk out to Glen Falloch.

METALLED ROAD		**LRT**	7 miles
TRAIL		**NO TRAIL**	3 miles
STARTING HEIGHT	150 ft.	**MAXIMUM HEIGHT**	1,320 ft.
HEIGHT CLIMBED	1,170 ft.		
BUS PICK-UP POINT	Lay by on A82 opposite Glen Falloch Farm		

Corrygoil to Glen Falloch (Walk 25)   Photograph by Billy Boyd

Corrygoil to Glen Falloch (Walk 25)   Photograph by Billy Boyd

Balquidder to Glen Ogle (Walk 21)   Photograph by Billy Boyd

Balquidder to Glen Ogle (Walk 21)   Photograph by Billy Boyd

WALKING

Walking is the exercise that needs no gymnasium.

It is the prescription without medicine,
the weight control without diet,
the cosmetic found in no beauty shop.

It is the tranquiliser without a pill,
the therapy without a psycho-analyst,
the fountain of youth that is no legend.

A walk is the holiday that costs you nothing.

HOTEL INFORMATION

The following establishments welcome bus parties for light refreshments. The proprietors would appreciate a telephone call prior to arrival; this would enable them to have sufficient staff available.

Location	Establishment	Telephone	Page
Ardlui	The Ardlui Hotel	01301 704243	81
Arrochar	The Pit Stop	0130 12570	82
Biggar	The Elphinstone Hotel	01899 20044	83
Comrie	The Royal Hotel	01764 70200	83
Callander	The Threshold	01877 330018	84
Drymen	The Pottery	01360 660458	85
Drymen	The Winnock	01360 60245	85
Dunkeld	The Pines	01350 727231	86
Dunkeld	The Royal Dunkeld	01350 727322	86
Fintry	The Clachan Hotel	01360 862 37	87
Moffat	The Rumblin' Tum	01683 20026	84
Moffat	Moffat House Hotel	01683 220039	88
Moffat	Adamson's	01683 221429	88
Pathhead	The Stair Arms	01875 320 929	87

The Green Welly Shop

Visit the Green Welly shop at Tyndrum in Perthshire
We are recognised as one of the West Highlands specialist outdoor shops.
Our staff are well qualified to give that important advice on what you should be wearing to contend with what can be the worst of British weather.
So if you are a Munro bagger, hill walker, walking the West Highland Way or if you simply love the great outdoors we'll have something to offer - that's for sure!

1. Boots - from Brasher, Gronell, Demon and Meindl.
2. Jackets - by Jack Wolfskin, Berghaus, Keela and Regatta.
3. Fleeces - from North Cape, Climbing 4, Berghaus.
4. Socks - By Thorlo, probably the best socks around.
5. Thermals - from Jack Wolfskin and North Cape.
6. Rucksacks - by Berghaus, Jack Wolfskin.

**Main stockists of Barbour,
Jack Wolfskin and Berghaus**

Green Wellies from Barbour, Aigle and Nokia

**We're only a 'phone call away and we'll
post anything anywhere.**

**Tel:	01838 400271
Fax:	018384 400330**

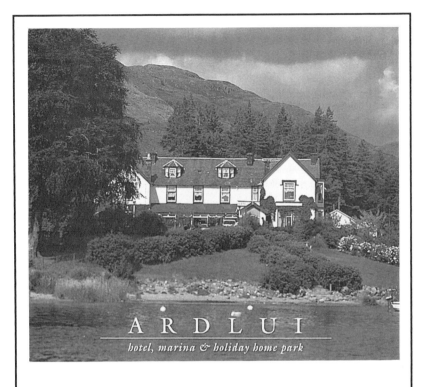

ARDLUI, Loch Lomond Dumbartonshire
Tel 01301 704243 Fax 01301 704268
Warm Relaxed & Friendly Atmosphere
Log Fire in Winter Months
Ferry Service to West Highland Way

walkers welcome

THE
PIT STOP DINER
ARROCHAR

TEL No 0130 12570

Extensive Fast Food Menu
Kiddies Menu
Clean & Friendly Surroundings
Seating for 54 Persons
Separate Take-Away Section
Ample Parking
Hikers, cyclists, fishermen and bikers
divers, families, buses and drivers

The PIT STOP
is
The place to **MEET** and **EAT**

The Stair Arms
Hotel & Restaurant
Ford, Pathhead Midlothian EH 37 5TX
Telephone: (01875) 320 277 Fax: (01875) 320 929

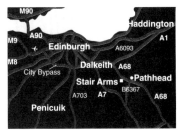

B & B

Function Room

Beer Garden

Bar Meals

The Clachan Hotel
Tom & Barbara Pollock
Main Street
FINTRY
Central Region
Scotland
G63 0XN   01360 860237

A seventeenth century hostelry used originally by the drovers
Tranquil setting facing on to the Fintry Hills
Bed and breakfast with *en suite* facilities
Large outdoor garden with barbecue facilities
Function suite available for private functions
Childrens play area*Pool / games room
Bar meals served Monday to Friday 12.00 to 2.30 pm
and 5.30 to 8.30 pm. Saturday 12.00 to 8.30 pm
Sunday 12.30 to 8.30 pm
*HIGH TEAS BOOKING ONLY

Moffat House Hotel

MOFFAT, DUMFRIESSHIRE. DG10 9HL   TEL: 01683 220039

ADAMSON'S
COFFEE HOUSE
BREAKFAST
served until 11a.m. only

FRUIT JUICE; EGGS AS YOU LIKE THEM – POACHED,
FRIED OR SCRAMBLED, WITH BACON, TOMATO AND HASH BROWN.
TEA/COFFEE WITH TOAST, BUTTER AND MARMALADE. ~ £

HOME BAKES

60 -67 HIGH ST TEL: 01683 221429

walkers welcome

Whitelaw's Coaches
Earls Tours
Group & Tours Coach Specialists

Head Office
Loch Park Industrial Estate
Stonehouse
Tel 01698 793506